Garsdale &

on the
Settle-Carlisle Railway

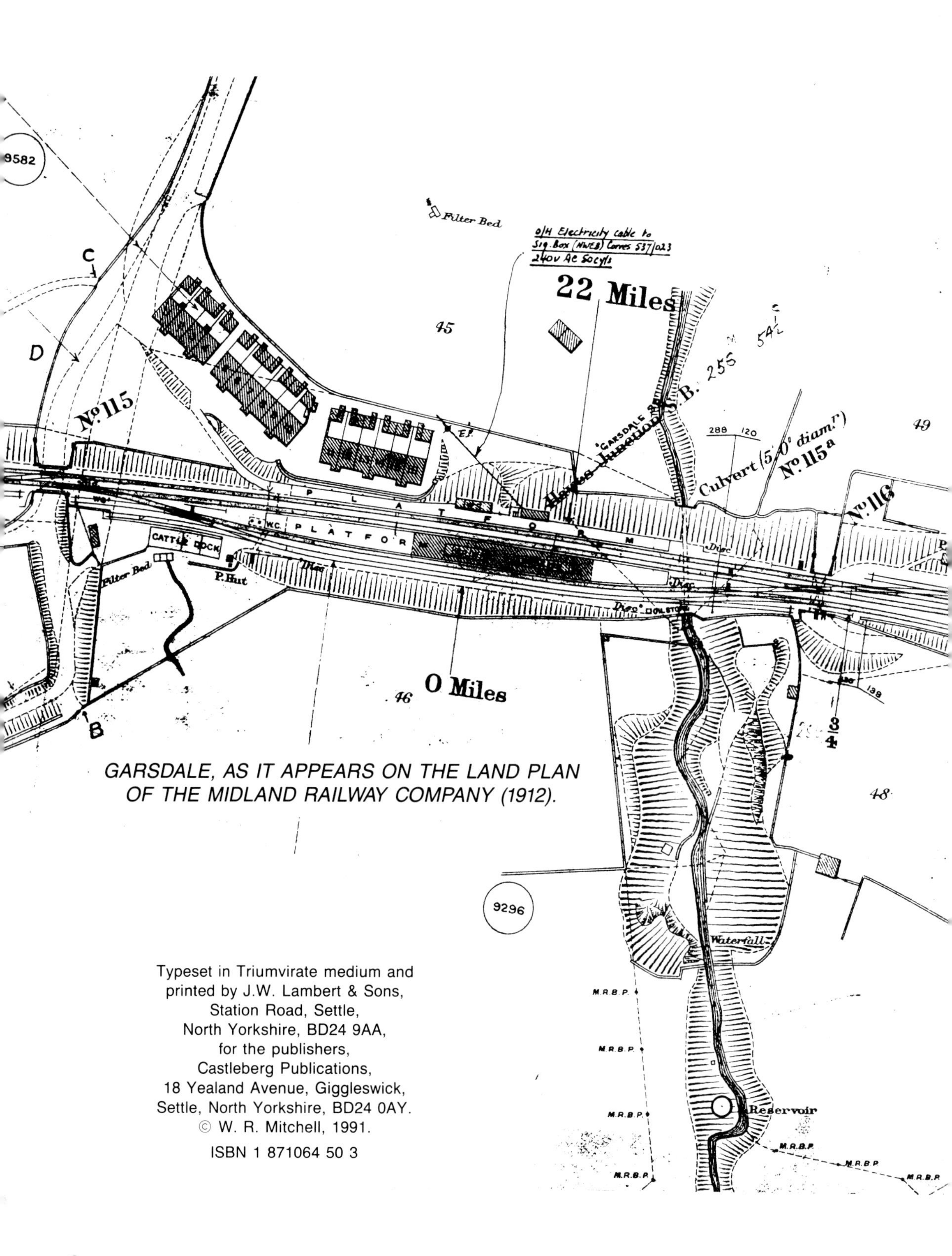

GARSDALE, AS IT APPEARS ON THE LAND PLAN OF THE MIDLAND RAILWAY COMPANY (1912).

Typeset in Triumvirate medium and
printed by J.W. Lambert & Sons,
Station Road, Settle,
North Yorkshire, BD24 9AA,
for the publishers,
Castleberg Publications,
18 Yealand Avenue, Giggleswick,
Settle, North Yorkshire, BD24 0AY.

ISBN 1 871064 50 3

Garsdale and Aisgill on the Settle-Carlisle Railway

by W. R. Mitchell
and Peter Fox

This booklet deals with what many consider to be the greatest section of the Settle-Carlisle line—the highest lengths—in an austere setting of fells and dales.

Above: Platelayers on track re-laying near Aisgill 50 years ago.

Below: Driver Cyril Patrickson hurries 5305 away from Garsdale with a short train for Skipton.

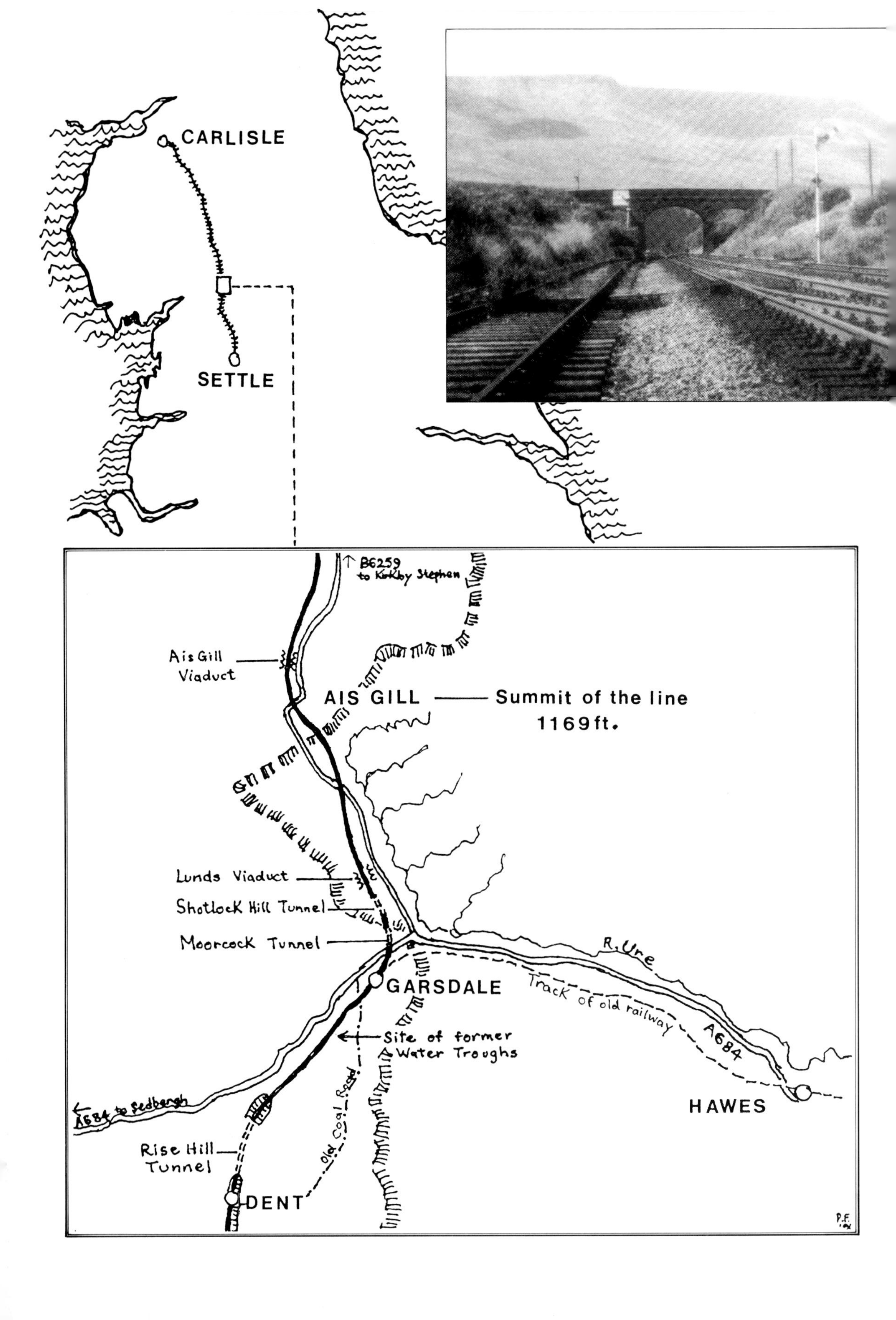
CARLISLE
SETTLE
B6259
to Kirkby Stephen
Ais Gill
Viaduct
AIS GILL
Summit of the line
1169ft.
Lunds Viaduct
Shotlock Hill Tunnel
Moorcock Tunnel
R. Ure
GARSDALE
Track of old railway
Site of former
Water Troughs
A684
A684 to Sedbergh
HAWES
Old Coal Road
Rise Hill
Tunnel
DENT
P.F.

Contents

Illustrations:

***Front cover**, top:* BR Guard at Garsdale (W.R. Mitchell). *Left:* Looking North from Garsdale station. *Bottom:* 46203 leaves Garsdale (photos: Peter Fox). ***Back cover**, top:* A Sprinter at Aisgill Bridge. *Bottom:* A well-filled platform at Garsdale (photos: Peter Fox).

Peter Fox: 1, 3 (bottom), 4, 10, 11, 12, 16, 18-20, 22, 24-27 (bottom), 30 (top), 31 (top), 32, 34, 38, 41, 44-48.

W.R. Mitchell: 3 (top), 8, 13-15, 17, 21, 23, 27 (top), 30 (bottom), 35-37, 39, 40, 42-43.

Pete Shaw: 6, 8, 31 (bottom).

S. Robinson: 28-29.

Ruth Annison: 33.

Knighton Collection: 5.

British Rail kindly made Land Plan maps available.

A Midland express passing Aisgill.

Foreword

by

Ruth Annison
Secretary, Wensleydale
Railway Association

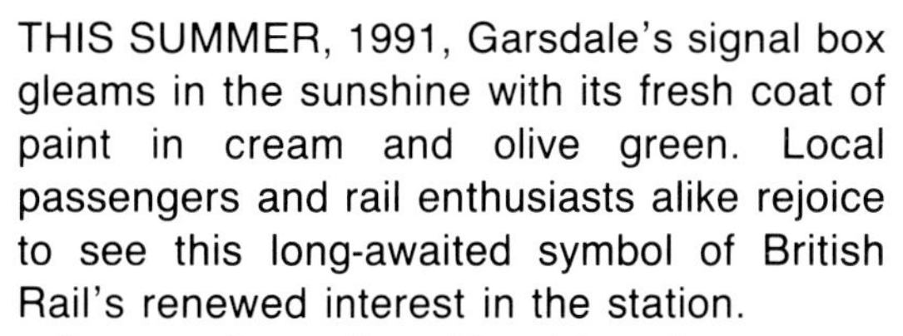

THIS SUMMER, 1991, Garsdale's signal box gleams in the sunshine with its fresh coat of paint in cream and olive green. Local passengers and rail enthusiasts alike rejoice to see this long-awaited symbol of British Rail's renewed interest in the station.

It was not ever thus. For sixteen long years, from 1970, the station was closed to passengers. The rails were there; the Permanent Way men still worked from a base in the old station buildings; motorists on the A684 sometimes spied a through train crossing Dandry Mire Viaduct, and from 1975 an occasional *Dalesrail* excursion train stopped at the station—but the Settle-Carlisle line was not a transport option for people in the area.

Then on 14th July, 1986, at just three weeks' notice, British Rail re-opened Garsdale and seven other stations on the Settle-Carlisle line. Residents of Garsdale village (three miles from the station) and the nearest small market town of Hawes (6 miles) and Sedbergh (10 miles) were astonished and delighted to find themselves re-connected to the national rail network.

However, the new train services coincided with deregulation of the buses, which finished off the already sketchy bus service between Hawes and Sedbergh. The total lack of public transport was difficult enough for local people, who could possibly arrange to drive or be driven to the station by car. It was a disaster for people *arriving* at the remote upland station, who might be stranded there without any of the facilities to be found within reach of an urban railway station such as refreshments, taxis and telephones.

John and Sheila Jeffreys, who run *Simonstone Hall Hotel,* near Hawes, heard about the problem and made a room available for a meeting to consider whether anything could be done. Eight of us met in the lovely panelled drawing room, with its spectacular views. It took us only a few minutes to decide that this beautiful landscape should not only be available to motorists. A linking bus service with the station was essential so that visitors could take advantage of the new train services to explore the surrounding countryside—the Howgill Fells, Upper Wensleydale and Swaledale, the "magic valley" of Mallerstang, Lady Anne Clifford's Trail and the long-distance Pennine Way.

"Alight at Garsdale" quickly became our motto, but how could we provide an instant bus service? The school holidays had just begun, trains were running but alas there wasn't even one minibus in Hawes, let alone a spare one! Yet, thanks to a prompt response by the Yorkshire Dales National

Park, Cumbria County Council, many individuals, parish councils, statutory and voluntary organisations and local businesses, services began and were advertised within a week of the station's re-opening.

In the following year, 1987, North Yorkshire County Council took over responsibility for the Garsdale-Hawes minibus service (as Cumbria had already done for the Garsdale-Sedbergh service) and British Rail increased the number of trains. More trains brought more passengers to the station, in spite of the fact that the future of the whole line was still under threat from long-standing closure proposals. Work also began to improve the appearance of the station under the Adopt-a-Station scheme organised by the Friends of the Settle-Carlisle line (FOSCL).

Although most of the stations had a team of keen volunteer painters and gardeners, the remoteness of Garsdale meant that no-one had yet come forward there. So Pete Shaw, secretary of FOSCL and living near Bradford, decided to make a start. Almost single-handed, he painted the outside of the station buildings—doors, windows, gutters and the bargeboards on the gables. After a chance meeting with him, members of Hawes Chamber of Trade volunteered to help with the work and in October 1987 the station won third prize in the Best Improved Station Competition.

There was never a master plan; the work just unrolled before us. As one task was completed, another became apparent. The "before and after" photographs that were taken over the months record how much has been done as, once again, volunteers were able to fulfil an important role in station affairs and show their support for British Rail's initiative in re-opening the station.

Since then, the popularity and convenience of rail travel in this part of the Yorkshire Dales National Park has been well-proven by the steady increase in passenger numbers. Residents of the area use Garsdale station for outward travel for shopping, family and social visits, business journeys, access to Leeds (via Shipley) and Manchester Airport and for holidays. Visitors use the station for access to the countryside and sight-seeing and many make repeat or regular visits.

Rail travel, over a fixed route, offers a balancing redress away from the honeypot areas where cars and crowds congregate. For outward travel to work and college, a secure year-round train service is now needed at the edges of the day to complete the usefulness of the station to the local community and fulfil the potential of yet more passengers.

Now the Wensleydale Railway Association, founded on 23rd May, 1990, under the chairmanship of County Councillor John Piper, is investigating the feasibility of re-opening the line between Northallerton, on the East Coast main line, and Garsdale station on the Settle-Carlisle. The project has attracted widespread interest and support because of the public transport and environmental benefits it would bring. Further information is given in a revised edition of Christine Hallas's book *The Wensleydale Railway* (Leading Edge Press, 1991).

It is now my special pleasure to welcome Bill Mitchell's fascinating book on *Garsdale and Aisgill.* As he wrote it and selected photographs, his attention has been focussed on a small but significant section of the Settle-Carlisle line, formerly called Hawes Junction and perhaps one day to be restored to that status!

Meanwhile the message about trains and linking minibus services is clear: every single passenger journey counts when service provision is reviewed. *Use it or lose it!*

Prince Charles and Lord Peel at Garsdale in June, 1991; they had just alighted from the Royal Train.

An Introduction

GARSDALE HEAD was transformed by the Midland Railway in the 1870s. What had been a remote farming community, served by dusty turnpike roads, became—through Midland brains and brass— a junction station, dealing with steam traffic on the Settle-Carlisle railway and the branch line into Wensleydale.

South of Garsdale, where small-time farmers had wrested a living from bare fellsides, Midland ingenuity and navvy muscles made cuttings, embankments, viaducts and tunnels. In 1907, water troughs were laid, each trough having a length of 1,670 ft and a total capacity of between 5,000 and 6,000 gallons. Needless to say, these were the highest water troughs on any rail system in Britain.

This is an area of superlatives. To the north of Garsdale—beyond the Moorcock (or Dandry Mire) Viaduct; beyond the Tunnels of Moorcock and Shotlock Hill—lies Aisgill, the highest point (1,169ft) of the Settle-Carlisle and, indeed, of any British railway. Aisgill is in true fell country, ringed with an awesome assembly of 2,000-footers. This area feels a back-draught from the Helm Wind, a cruel blast, brewed up around High Cup Nick.

The Helm Wind races along the East Fellside, its presence on the Pennines being indicated by a long cloud, straight as a brushshaft. The Helm, which some people assert has never crossed the river Eden, used to blow cobs of coal from a railway fireman's shovel!

I am one of those many happy people who remember Garsdale station when it had a full time staff and dealt with steam-hauled traffic both on the Settle-Carlisle and the Hawes branch lines. (My godfather, a driver based at Skipton, sometimes carried out snow-clearing duties on that branch).

Garsdale was the place where you might post a letter in a VR postbox, the plate of which had the magical name of ''Garsdale Station''. The almost-legendary *Bonnyface,* a Bradford-Hawes express, was a familiar sight. The locomotive's face was not especially bonny—it was, indeed, streaked with soot—but the permanent way men always liked to see it on its return journey, when it reminded them that the working day was almost over.

I have had to rely on others for memories of some distinctive aspects of life at Garsdale Head. Dances were held in the Tank House, with a buffet available in an adjacent wheelless coach. Garsdale had its Engine Shed. It was not as grand as the Midland construction committee had originally planned. The Shed people recalled to me was that which replaced the original structure, burnt down in 1917. An Engine Shed did give a special status to Garsdale.

Entertaining stories were told of the turntable. In 1900, a gale blew so furiously that a locomotive which had been put on the turntable was spun like a top for two hours, until the movement was slowed by spilling sand into the centre well. That was the story—confirmed when I saw a telegraphic message, sent at the time, briefly reporting on the incident. (The traverser has been sold to the Keighley and Worth Valley railway, so that they might put their own turntable back into use).

Most times, Garsdale station is devoid of people. It is then hard to picture this high Pennine railway station as it was reported to be prior to 1914, when almost all the trains were double-headed and the long-suffering signalmen found themselves "cluttered up" with light engines, the drivers of which were anxious to return to their bases.

Garsdale folk, most of whom worked for the railway, formed a proud and independent community for almost a century. When I visited Garsdale in 1991 the old place was looking well, having been hastily re-decorated in advance of a visit by high-ranking politicians. Prince Charles, who has a good friend in the Dales, is no stranger to this isolated Pennine railway station.

This booklet, *Garsdale and Aisgill* has been devised to put on record stories relating to the rise and decline of the only junction station on the Settle-Carlisle railway. Once known as Hawes Junction and Garsdale, it was never very large, though most strategically placed. Garsdale, opened in August, 1876, was provided with three small stone buildings which, elsewhere, would be described as "waiting shelters". A photograph of 1900 shows that one of them was adorned with a wooden canopy to cheat the Pennine rain.

Hawes Junction and Garsdale—a vintage photograph, with the station awning still in place.

A panoramic view looking from Lunds towards Wild Boar Fell and Aisgill. The railway cottages, the box-type crossover bridge and Shotlock Tunnel are all clearly visible. No. 4472 *Flying Scotsman* rounds the curve on a "steam special".

The Midland Influence

A visitor to Garsdale Head who has travelled up Wensleydale sees evidence of the ordinary life of the Dales—one or two farms, a large house which has evolved from a shooting lodge and, of course, *The Moorcock,* which stands where the Hawes-Sedbergh road is joined by that traversing Mallerstang on its way to Kirkby Stephen. All are connected to each other, and to everywhere else in the Dales, by an intricate pattern of drystone walls.

Elsewhere, the Garsdale Head structures are of the Railway Age, dating from 1869-76. An immense Victorian-style railway bridge spans the road. The name Moorcock Cottages is given to a short row of terraced homes. (The Midland Railway like the name "cottages"; they also wisely arranged for some of the walls to be reinforced with slate to deflect the wet winds).

On the opposite side of the road, and just beyond the bridge—where North Yorkshire gives way to Cumbria—stands Mount Zion, a Primitive Methodist chapel built in the 1870s. The voluntary builders included a few railway navvies.

To the left of the road are two massive embankments and, between them, the viaduct built to cross the wettest parts of Dandry Mire. From here, Garsdale station's cluster of buildings is seen to be clinging to the hillside. Also in view is the line of the old Coal Road, a former packhorse route, which takes an undulating course to a bridge spanning the railway at Dent station.

Northwards from Garsdale stands further dramatic evidence of "navvy time"—Moorcock Tunnel, Lunds Viaduct (made from stone taken from the immediate vicinity) and an incongruous metal footbridge beside the drove road leading into Grizedale. I cannot imagine local people using the footbridge, but it is now a splendid vantage point when photographing "steam specials".

As related, the railway reaches its summit at Aisgill.

For Fast Traffic

The Settle-Carlisle was planned as a fast, all-weather route to Scotland, a middle route between two keen competitors: the *North Western* and the *North Eastern* Railways. Local traffic was not the primary consideration. The Midland must have its share of the lucrative Scottish trade.

This was the last railway in Britain to be constructed in a time-honoured way, with an abundance of labour and simple implements. In truth, steam-cranes were employed to lift stones on to the viaduct, a new-fangled explosive called dynamite had become popular and as the weary years of digging out cuttings went on, the Midland experimented with a machine to dispose of a geological mush called "boulder clay", which lay thickly on the hillside.

Settle-Carlisle must have a ruling gradient that did not exceed 1 in 100. Its trains must be able to run safely at a speed of up to 90 miles an hour, by day or night, in dry or wet conditions, through the long days of summer and on short, crisp winter days when the Pennines glistened with frost.

These objectives were gloriously, and expensively, achieved. Six thousand men were set to work, the structures being made of local stone, with much Limestone being used in North Ribblesdale and New Red Sandstone giving a rosy glow to stations in the Eden Valley. The lines' gradients ensured that they crossed Aisgill Moor, at well over 1,000 feet, on a virtually level stretch.

It had been an engineering challenge that John Crossley could not forego. He, the Midland's engineer-in-chief, delayed his retirement to see the work through. Crossley died in 1878, which was not long after the line was opened to passenger traffic.

In the Wet

The weather is an important aspect of this account of life on the Northern Pennines. Among the high fells, the weather is transient. Sunshine is rapidly followed by a shower—and that shower might last half a day. Summers tend to be cool and cloudy. Winters are almost unbearably long to anyone like a farmer with a living to earn.

On days when there is something of railway interest to be observed or photographed, the Weather Clerk is inclined to tease the many

An artist's view of Garsdale water tower.

The majesty of steam at Aisgill. In the picture is LMS No. 5305, attacking Aisgill in brilliant sunshine after a sudden snowstorm, March, 1980. The location is one beloved of train photographers and was often used by Bishop Treacy.

photographers, contriving that a blizzard rages where 10 minutes before the sun was shining from a cloudless sky. Yet the railway fans who arrive with cameras and tape recorders are an indomitable breed, not to be put off by snarling winds or a foot or two of snow.

One day, at Garsdale, a hillside which had been whitened by hail suddenly turned patchily black when the toot of a "steam special" was heard. Dozens of photographers threw off the waterproofs under which they had sheltered and prepared to record the train's arrival!

It was on an unpromising day—a wet, dull, and, astonishingly for Garsdale, a calm day—that I secured my favourite sequence of a locomotive at Garsdale. A "special", stopping for water, was enveloped in steam for a few moments after moving off. For a few seconds, there was billowing whiteness, and then the engine appeared to view, eerily, through the smoke. It was like a transformation scene at a pantomime.

Across Aisgill Moor

At Aisgill, the county boundary is crossed and the highest mainline railway summit in England is traversed under the blue-black gaze of Wild Boar Fell. (Some two-thirds of the famous railway lie in the county of Cumbria). Rail travellers see the enamelled notices proclaiming the place and altitude—and little else of railway note.

Aisgill has been stripped of its Victorian features. The refuge sidings have been lifted; the signal box in which I had a welcome cup of coffee on a cold day has been moved to a preserved railway in Derbyshire. At Aisgill, passengers have a momentary view of Hellgill Force, a splendid waterfall, which after responding to heavy rain cries out like a prophet in the wilderness.

Aisgill Viaduct was flung across a deep gill from which comes the roar of tumbling water. A cool, humid atmosphere favours the growth of flowers and ferns and the beck trips down a natural rock staircase under one of the four arches of Aisgill Viaduct, which is at an elevation of 1,167 feet above sea level.

The Hawes Branch

The Wensleydale branch closed in March, 1959, leaving in regular use only 10 of the original 40 levers in the Garsdale signal box, which is situated on the "down" platform. On a summer day in 1953, I was the only passenger for the Wensleydale train, so the driver invited me to join him and the fireman on the footplate! They were making last minute preparations for the departure of the 10-50. Eventually, above the hiss of escaping steam, came the blast of the guard's whistle.

Levers were pulled. Wheels turned. The engine clutched at the rails and the journey began, to continue under the steely gaze of horned sheep and their lambs. The driver gave a toot to lift the spirits of farmers, then occupied with the tedious and unsavoury job of hand-forking "muck" and spreading it in the meadows.

Washing Day at the Railway Cottages, Garsdale.

Victorian letterbox, marked "Garsdale Station", which was built into the front outer wall of a platform building.

These two pages hold details of the layout of Garsdale Station (from the Midland Land Plan, 1912). The photographs: this page—The Tank House, in the process of being dismantled. Opposite page: A 1930s view of the Tank House and the old Midland coach used as a refreshment room. The locomotive is an ex-Midland Railway 4-4-0.

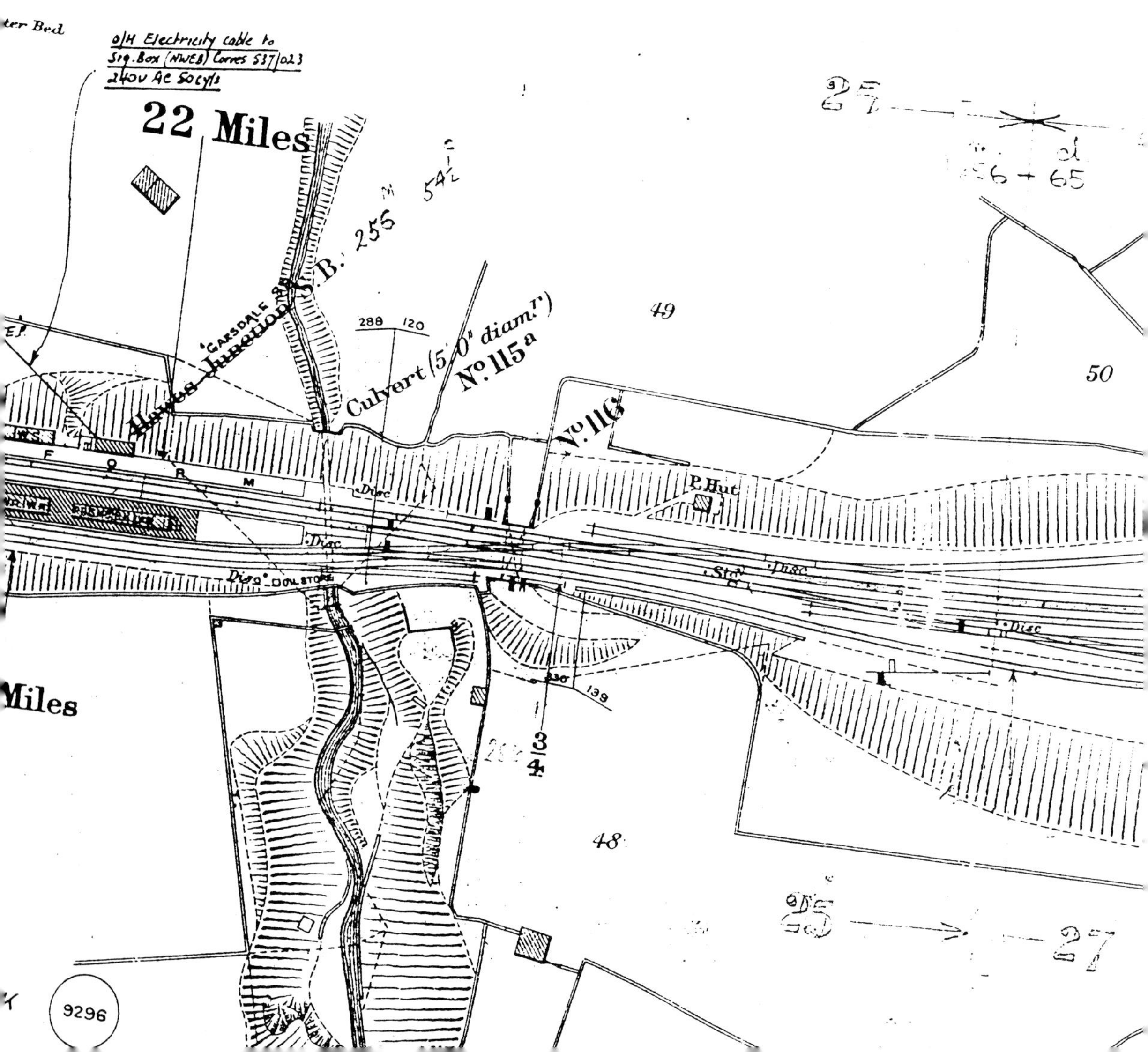

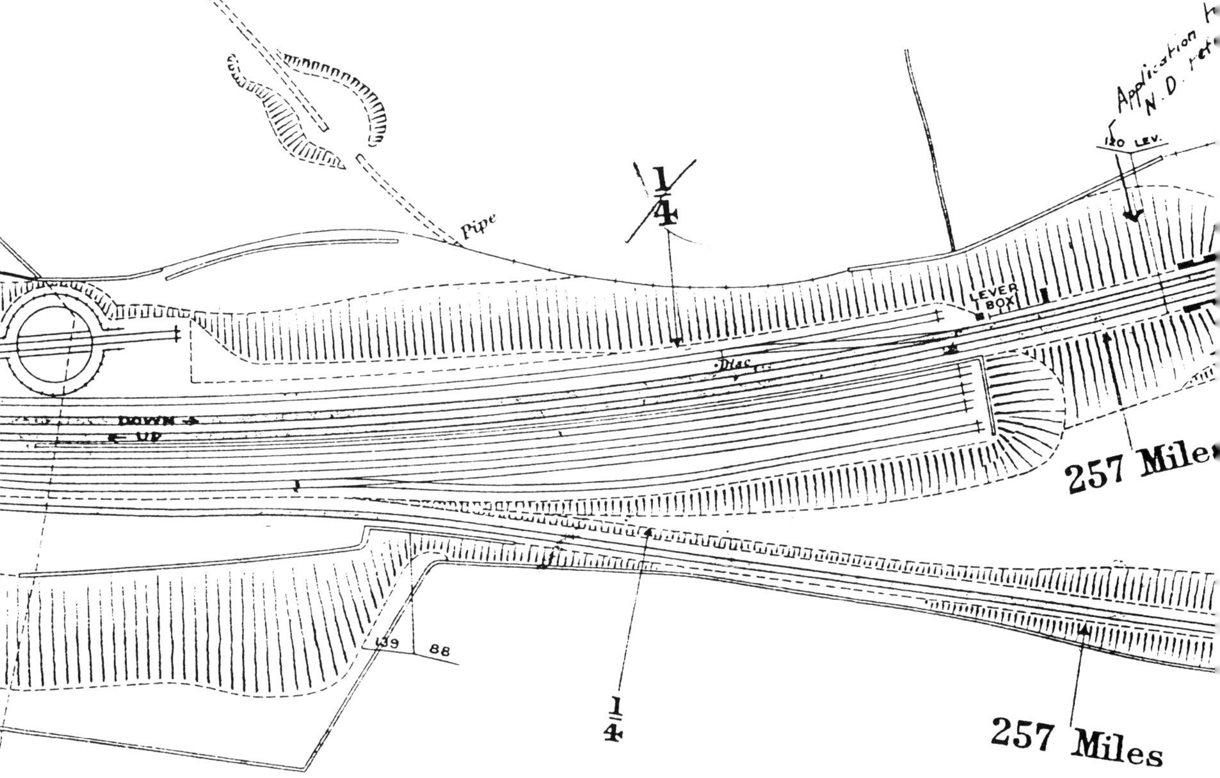
Pipe
1/4
LEVER BOX
Disc
DOWN
UP
120 LEV.
257 Miles
139
88
1/4
257 Miles

Studies of Garsdale Station as it is today. Settle-Carlisle platforms are relatively low for modern rolling stock, hence the steps provided *(bottom, right).*

Garsdale Before the Railway

FOR CENTURIES, the goods which passed between the far-flung communities of the Dales were borne on the backs of pack horses, which followed a pattern of ancient tracks. Then came the turnpike trusts, who established and maintained routes on which tolls were charged.

One such route was that from Hawes through Mallerstang to Kirkby Stephen. At Collier Holme, about a mile beyond Appersett, the turnpike road (which is also the line of the present road) swung west, forsaking the old coach route, known as the High Way, which made a rapid ascent to Cotter Clints. Here for about a mile traffic moved on a natural ledge of limestone high above the valleys.

Lady Anne Clifford, a 17th century celebrity, traversed the High Way more than once. In 1663, when she was conveyed from Skipton to Appleby, she noted in her diary:". . . and the next day I went over Cotter, which I lately repaired, and I came into the Pendragon Castle . . ."

Hell Gill bridge was old in 1675, when it was repaired at a cost of £3.10s. Spanning a deep gorge which is the cradle of the River Eden, the structure was listed as a County Bridge in 1825, the year in which the present bridge was constructed. It was to be maintained by the highway authorities of Yorkshire and Westmorland.

At the back-end, when Brough Hill Fair was held, the road was busy indeed. The stock sold at Brough Hill included 10,000 Scotch cattle, most of which were then driven southwards as good beef on the hoof, to become food for the urban masses.

The High Way is now a walkers' route, often wrapped in cloud. Arthur Raistrick, the Dales historian, with whom I had many stimulating conversations about the upper Dales, mentioned that the antiquary of the High Way could be assessed by reference to local farm names to which *"High"* is attached. Those names include High Dike and High Way (on the stretch to Lunds) and High Hall near Washer Gill. The Horse Paddock, a small enclosure, was where pack animals, temporarily relieved of their loads, spent the night.

Another ancient route much used by pack animals was The Galloway Gate, which followed the Coal Road from Dent to Garsdale Head, leaving Garsdale at Knows Foot Bridge, just

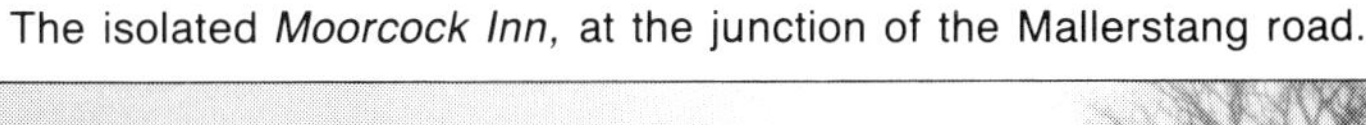

The isolated *Moorcock Inn,* at the junction of the Mallerstang road.

below the railway station. From here, it ascended Garsdale Common to attain 1,760 ft at Cowgill Head. The name "Galloway" relates to a sturdy type of pony. (The Gate was a branch of a famous old drove road from Scotland).

The Coal Road, well-used by Settle-Carlisle enthusiasts wanting a quick route between the stations of Dent and Garsdale, served the pits of the Garsdale Colliery. Rough tracks led from it to the shafts that were sunk to connect with the seams of hard, brittle coal found in the Yoredale Series of rocks. The Settle-Carlisle line brought about the closure of the Colliery by transporting a better class of coal from South Yorkshire.

The present road down Mallerstang came into being during the turnpike period. Work began in 1825 to provide a link between Kirkby Stephen and the Sedbergh-Kirkby Lonsdale turnpike. By October, 1829, it had been "properly made and fit for the reception of travellers." It was then continued to Hawes and Gayle, in Wensleydale.

The Moorcock, named after the red grouse, has a strategic position where the Hawes-Sedbergh road is joined by that running down Mallerstang to Kirkby Stephen. The inn's isolated position ensured that it was mentioned on many general maps of England.

A Clear Head of

am at Dandry Mire, Garsdale

The Men who Built the Railway

GARSDALE and Aisgill were part of Contract No. 2 (Dent Head to Kirkby Stephen), which the Midland awarded to Messrs Benton and Woodiwiss. This firm also had the contract for the branch line to Hawes.

The contractors opened up quarries for the viaducts and prepared to drive a tunnel through Rise Hill. They reckoned on hiring 1,400 men for the whole contract, and managed by and large to keep this number, though the turnover of workers was tremendous as men left for pleasanter work. It was estimated in 1872 that a total of about 17,000 men had "jacked up".

F.S. Williams, a Victorian historian of the Midland Railway, mentioned that every "tip wagon" used by the contractor had to be brought by road up from Sedbergh, the cost of moving each wagon being a guinea. A hundred such wagons were needed.

In June, 1873, a visitor was given a lift on a locomotive bearing "the aristocratic name of Lorne." He was shown the progress of the work at the tunnel. On the summit, as in Garsdale itself, were many contractors' huts. A 600 yard long tramway connected the vicinity of the tunnel with the Garsdale road. "It is by this steep pathway that all the railway material for this portion of the line is drawn up by a rope worked by steam power," he remarked.

No time was lost by the contractor in tackling Dandry Mire, just north of the site of Garsdale station, where an embankment was proposed. "The miry state of the ground has given the contractors and managers an inconceivable amount of trouble and labour. Tipping went on for more than two years, and instead of a solid embankment being formed, the peat yielded to the weight of the filling to such an extent that it rose on each side of the line in the form of a high bank—in some places 15ft.

Finding after more than 250,000 cubic yards had been tipped that the bog would not sustain the weight of the clay and stone used for filling up, it was decided to make a six-arch viaduct in the deepest part of the moss. Each arch would be of 45 ft span. The greatest depth of a pier was 53 ft. For nearly the whole length it averaged from 45ft to 50ft foundation to top of the peat. The peat varied from 5 ft to 15 ft., the greater portion of which had to be dug out before the embankment which is to join the viaduct could be formed.

The new bridge spanning the Sedbergh-Hawes road, at the north end of the embankment was reported to have "a lofty and well-turned arch with neatly-dressed facings. . . Near the bridge there are some neat (contractor's) huts, some of which are slated and others had whitewashed sides and roofs. On this and No. 3 contract, most of the huts are whitewashed all over, while the huts on No 1 contract were gas tarred."

A writer for *Wildman's Household Almanack* toured the line in 1874 and found much of what he saw around Garsdale was "dreary". He wrote: "The Moorcock is an inn situated in the dreariest part of the line, quite an isolated spot before the railway was commenced." The engineering problems at Dandry Mire were mentioned, as were those caused when excavating a large cutting in an area smeared with boulder clay. "It contains without the slips 215,000 cubic yards."

This scribe referred to the *Moorcock* as an out-of-the-way place, where it was with extreme difficulty that labour could be obtained, "although comfortable huts are provided and high wages given here." So to Aisgill. "There are a few more dreary cuttings before the summit of the railway is at Ais Gill Moor. . . Near this spot three rivers take their rise, the Eden, the Ure and the Swale. The railway follows the first-named to Carlisle."

In October, 1875, when the Settle-Carlisle had been opened for goods traffic, Aisgill and Lunds viaducts were reported to be complete, except for their parapet walls. Aisgill had been spanned by a structure that was 66 ft high, with 45 ft span. The 99 yard long viaduct had been given four spans. "The gill on the south side is very romantic and on account of its overhanging rocks, it presents to the eye a very bold appearance. The stone which is dug from the hill on the high side is lifted to the viaduct by a steam jib crane."

Some of the Victorian residents of Garsdale railway cottages photographed on the platform.

In that autumn of 1875, only a little trimming at the entrances remained before the completion of the Shotlock and Moorcock Tunnels. Dandry Mire was still giving trouble. "Since the line was opened for goods traffic, it has sunk as much as four feet within the twenty-four hours. Old sleepers have to be put in to keep up the metals. The goods trains have to pass over at a greatly diminished speed. A large number of men were at work raising a side tip to give weight and stability sufficient to resist the pressure of the bank."

At the *Moorcock* "a little on the east side of the embankment, six neat cottages have been built for workmen whose services will be constantly needed on the line."

Masons were at work on the walls of the platforms and at some of the cottages. "The works, when completed, will form a small village . . . It is reported that a large reservoir will be made to supply the engines and other places with water. The Hawes branch is not in a forward state on account of some deviations in the line as marked out at the first, and the difficulty in coming to a proper settlement about the land."

Victorian writers loved to include in their work some lyrical passages, and this was no exception. "At Moorcock there is a considerable curve to the south-west, and as one travelled on the lofty banks of Garsdale (the writer was heading south) there was a fine view of the deep and narrow valley below. This paradise of peace and plenty among the hills opened out beautifully in the direction of Sedbergh.

"The little farmsteads dotting the green fields, the winding stream with its rocky banks fringed with trees and shrubs, and the zig-zag fences enclosing the meadow and pastureland, with lowering hills on three sides, was a landscape of rare beauty, even when seen in the shade."

An artist's impression of an LMS 4F locomotive taking water in the bay platform at Garsdale. This was a common practice especially for freight trains after tackling the climb to Aisgill.

Left: The Primitive Methodist Chapel.
Bottom, right: Midland "Gothic"—cottages built for the "railway servants".

Midland Architecture near the "Moorcock"

After leaving Garsdale, the line curves south-westwards, on the fellside, the Midland taking advantage of a short length of level track to instal water troughs—the highest in the land. Our photograph shows No. 45596 *Bahamas* taking the *Royal Scotsman* southwards on a tour of England in April, 1991.

Hawes Junction and Garsdale

Garsdale, with only the through tracks remaining.

FEW RAILWAY stations have had their names changed more often than Garsdale. It was first referred to (1872) as Hawes Junction. It then became Hawes Junction and Garsdale, and later it was Garsdale for Hawes. The sensible title of Garsdale was brought into use in 1932.

Garsdale, when viewed from near the little Methodist Chapel on the Sedbergh road, still looks incongruous in an area of small farms, field barns and endless walls. A small passenger exchange station was proposed. Exchange sidings would be provided for goods traffic, also "a steam shed to hold 24 engines with adequate water supply and for the housing of the staff, 30 cottages will be wanted."

Two years later, a much smaller scheme was outlined—the building of a shed for 12 engines, "with tank to hold 36,000 gallons of water", and 20 cottages for the workers. In 1877, the construction committee minutes record that "the Hawes Junction engine establishment has been much altered and the work reduced." In truth, the Company had overspent, leading to some economies during the closing stages of building the railway.

The North Eastern Railway, which usually worked the service to Hawes, used the Garsdale shed, which—as related—was burnt down in 1917. Much damage was caused to the 0-4-0T that was being stabled there. The shed was rebuilt and finally closed in 1939.

The buildings which would be used by passengers were unimpressive, being of the "platform shelter" type. No goods shed was provided. At most stations, the Stationmaster was housed in some style at a detached house, but Garsdale's Stationmaster was expected to live in one of the terrace houses.

Garsdale station saw the evidence of Wensleydale's quarry boom. East Lancashire was thriving and vast numbers of flagstones and building stones were being sent from quarries such as that at Burtersett, via Hawes and Garsdale, for the new houses and mills.

All the surplus livestock went by rail. The lamb trade began in August, when a special train left for Manchester on Monday evenings. Special trains for sheep were needed to handle stock from the November sales. Garsdale had the usual county station facilities for livestock—the holding pens for cattle and sheep. Mr Bell Pratt went into Scotland for cows. Another Mr Pratt, of Burtersett, who was a dealer in farmstock with many contacts in Scotland, was frequently driven by horse and trap to catch the "Scotch express" at Garsdale.

His daughter relates that one frosty morning, when she had simply put a long warm coat over her nightdress, she was returning through Appersett when a local lady she knew waved her down, invited her into the house and gave her a hot drink!

Above: In busier times, 4F No. 44324 simmers quietly near Aisgill box on a summer's evening.
Below: The small shop at Garsdale intercepted passengers. Notice the Brooke Bond Tea sign. In the background, the *Duchess of Hamilton* waits to enter Garsdale while a Class 40 diesel hauls the Engineer's inspection "special".

Local farmers collected the animals from the station or they employed a drover like Tommy Byker, of Gayle. The cattle, arriving at Garsdale on a late train, were walked through the night to their ultimate destination.

When I first visited Garsdale, over 40 years ago, the Stationmaster showed me a battered register of lost property which gave an indication of changing fashions in the Dales. Entries under 1895, the first year this record was kept, categorised as "lost" a whip and a retriever dog.

In 1896, a basket of rhubarb and a parcel of clogs were among the entries. A fishing net was "lost" in 1901, a carpet stretcher in 1902, a white muff in 1905, a gold mounted umbrella in both 1909 and 1910, and "two butcher's knives" in 1920. Two items from the page headed 1923 were "tin box containing bits of linseed cake" and "three ploughshares".

Only one train from the Midland Region clattered down the branch line, and that was the 12.46 from Bradford to Hawes, the one known to the railwaymen as "Bonnyface". I have heard it referred to as the only train from Hawes to Garsdale that ran on time. As the distance between the two places is less than six miles, keeping to the timetable would not prove difficult.

A train is said to have been driven from Garsdale to Hawes in six minutes. The passengers did not seem to mind, the alternative transport being horse and wagonette—or Shank's Pony.

Atmosphere at G

With visibility down to a few yards, as low cloud and mist envelop this high-lying station, an old-time feeling is evoked. The steam whirs round the driver, Cyril Patrickson, as he chats with Peter Fox. Meanwhile, the thirsty locomotive takes water from a reservoir set on the hillside.

dale

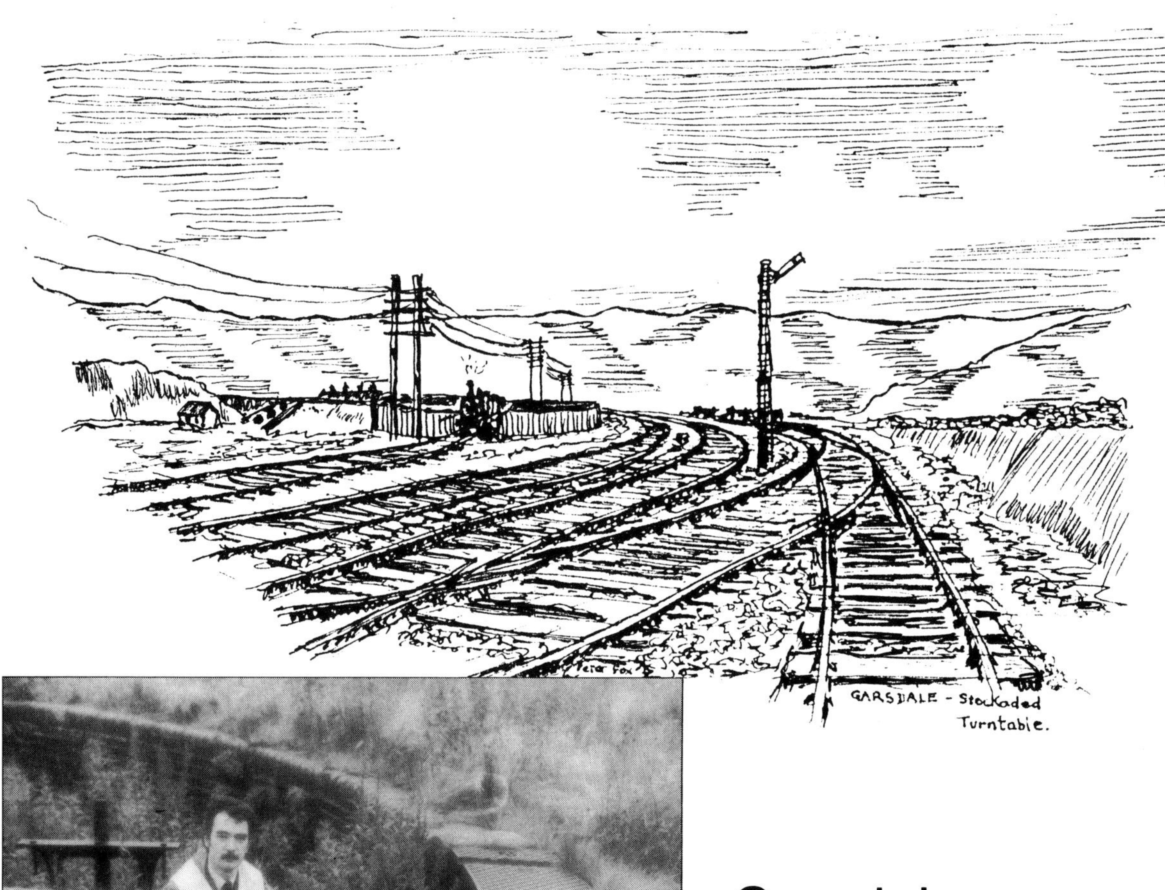

Garsdale Turntable

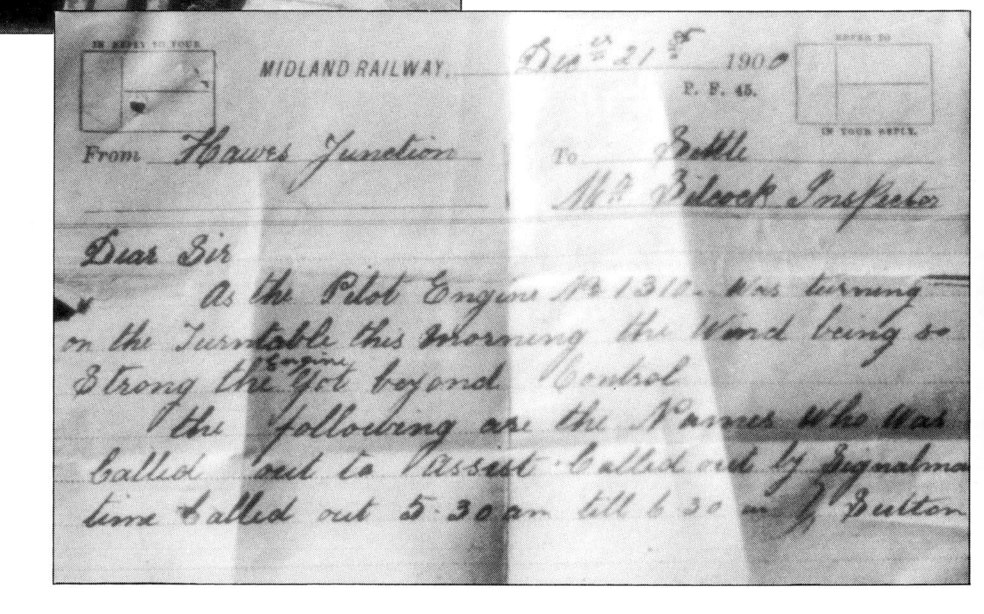

MIDLAND RAILWAY, Dec 21st 1900

P. F. 45.

From Hawes Junction

To Settle

Mr Bilcock Inspector

Dear Sir

As the Pilot Engine No 1310 was turning on the Turntable this morning the Wind being so Strong the Engine Got beyond Control

the following are the Names who Was Called out to Assist Called out by Signalman time Called out 5.30 am till 6.30 am J Sutton

Opposite page, centre: Paul Holden, now Line Manager, in the turntable at Garsdale when its future was under discussion. *Opposite page, bottom:* A copy of the ganger's report on an incident in which a locomotive spun out of control on the famous turntable. *This page, top:* A drawing of the Midland Railway 2-4-0, the type involved in the incident. *Below:* Garsdale turntable being lifted out for removal to the Keighley and Worth Valley Railway in February, 1989. The breakdown train is headed by Class 31 No. 31200.

A Lost Locomotive

Dandry Mire, showing the viaduct and *(right)* part of the embankment from which the loco chimney was recovered. (The train crossing the viaduct is Sir Nigel Gresley).

MY OLD FRIEND Dick Fawcett (Rabbity Dick), who began work on the Settle-Carlisle in 1932, being given a job in the "slip and drainage" gang, recalled in his book *Ganger, Guard and Signalman on the Settle-Carlisle Railway* the new (and annoying) experience of living beside a main line.

He was a light-sleeper who moved from a quiet house to No 2 Moorcock Cottages. "I would just drop off to sleep. . . when the trains of the night were coming at me from both directions. The 'up' trains were the worst, because they came so suddenly out of the deep cutting at the south end of Moorcock Tunnel. . . but I got used to it after a while".

Terry Sykes and Helen Smith, on re-reading Dick's memories, came across his remembrance of how, as a young ganger, he heard of a loco driver who made an error of judgement, which led to his engine toppling down the embankment near Dandry Mire Viaduct. All efforts to recover the engine failed. It was eventually covered by ballast and rubble. Dick mentioned having seen the chimney protruding from the embankment in the mid-1930s.

Terry and Helen secured BR permission to visit the area and here, on their third visit with a metal detector, they got a strong signal from what turned out to be the locomotive chimney, which (unhappily for their prospects of finding a complete locomotive) was lying upside down!

However, they did prod all round the chimney with a four foot steel rod and they had the loan of a Thorn EMI magnetic detector, with a range of nine feet. Nothing large and metallic was found.

So the old story of the "lost" locomotive must have been a spoof. The re-discoverers have written: "To the Victorian perpetrators of the joke, many, many thanks. It's been a fascinating project and, even in the mud and rain, very enjoyable."

The chimney has been put on show in the waiting room at Appleby, awaiting the time when the Hawes branch from Garsdale is reopened and it might be displayed locally.

Helen Smith and Terry Sykes with the loco chimney recovered from the embankment. The chimney was carried to a van under Dandry Mire viaduct with the aid of two friends and a sturdy pole. The chimney's new home is the platform at Appleby station.

Drawings of the two locomotives which were hauling the northbound Scotch express that crashed into the rear of two light engines at Lunds, just north of Garsdale, on December 24, 1910. It is said that the conscientious but over-worked signalman said to a colleague when he realised what had happened: ''Go tell the Stationmaster I've wrecked the Scotch express.''

Two Disastrous Accidents

THE TWO most famous accidents on the Settle-Carlisle occurred not far from Garsdale station. They had similar ingredients—wild weather, errors relating to signalling, in one case forgetfulness by the signalman and in the other pre-occupation by an engine driver. The consequence, in each case, was a collision, fire and loss of life.

The seeds of the first disaster were sown in the summer of 1910, with the closure of one of the Garsdale signal boxes, which concentrated all the signalling into one box. A single person had responsibility for what at times could be a most complex situation, such as would be undreamed of today, when traffic is comparatively light.

Signalman Alfred Sutton's work involved regular trains, plus many small pilot

locomotives jockeying for position before returning to their bases. It was the dark, wild morning of Christmas Eve, 1910.

The remaining signal box was on the "down" platform (where, indeed, it is today). Sutton's term of duty had begun at 8 p.m. on the previous evening. It was now after 5 a.m. Two light engines, Nos. 448 and 548, were to return together to their base in Carlisle.

At about 5.20, Sutton dealt with a "down" special express. When it had cleared the junction, he signalled the two light engines to move, which they did, halting at the advanced starter signal. Sutton's intention was to wait until the special express had cleared Aisgill, before signalling the two small engines to proceed northwards.

As the engines crossed over to the "down" line at about 5.21 a.m., Sutton accepted an "up" goods train from Aisgill box. He then began the task of shifting the three other light engines, two of which had come of the turntable and were to return to Leeds; the third having gone to a lie-by siding.

Events now crowded in on each other. Aisgill informed Sutton that the "down" special had cleared the section. At that time he was concerned with the despatch of the two Leeds engines, Nos 247 and 249. He appeared to have overlooked the two pilot engines which were waiting at the advanced starter for the signal to proceed to Carlisle. The footplate men, though somewhat delayed, do not appear to have taken any action to let him know they were still there. And it was a dark, wild morning.

At 5.29 a.m., the "up" goods from Aisgill passed the box. Aisgill promptly offered Sutton another. He asked Aisgill to let him know how close the goods train was, as he was anxious to get the two Leeds engines away in advance. Aisgill requested that the goods train should have precedence; so it was accepted. The time was 5.32 a.m..

Signalman Sutton had much on his mind.He had to cope with normal traffic, light engines, arranging a relief for one of the Leeds enginement and with arrangements for two engines from Hellifield that stood on the turntable line.

Enter—the "down" Scotch express!

This train had two engines, the first one a

pilot. In the carriages were 56 passengers, a sleeping car attendant and passenger guard, en route from St. Pancras to Glasgow and running a little late. The train was accepted by Sutton. As the second "up" goods ran past his box, he offered the express on to Aisgill. It was accepted. Sutton lowered all his down signals to let it through.

The drivers of the Carlisle light engines responded to the green light with short whistles which would not carry far in those wild conditions. They set off for Carlisle. The Scotch express—about 16 minutes late—was overhauling them at speed.

The inevitable collision occurred at Lunds Viaduct, just north of Moorcock Tunnel. The two light engines were pushed forward about 190 yards. The two leading coaches of the Scotch express were telescoped and the hot coals from the engine ignited gas in the cylinders kept beneath the coaches.

Twelve people died from the impact and the fire that followed, which consumed the whole train excepting the last two brake vans. At the inquiry, the hapless Sutton was censured for forgetting about the two light engines. The drivers of the light engines were considered remiss in that after a certain period of waiting they should have gone to the signal box and waited until the signal was lowered.

Within three years, another serious accident in the Garsdale/Aisgill area created alarm because of similarities with the Lunds affair. On September 2, 1913, a sleeper from Glasgow and Stranraer came to a half a mile north of Aisgill summit. The driver of the heavy train had requested a pilot engine, but none was available. The driver was also having trouble through using inferior coal.

Behind the sleeper came a night train from Inverness and Edinburgh, the crew of which was also having a struggle to keep moving. They had poor quality coal. So pre-occupied were they in trying to get sufficient steam, they over-ran the Mallerstang signals, colliding with the rear of the standing train. Fire broke out. The death toll was 14.

Two photographs on these pages are from a large collection taken at the time of the accidents near Aisgill. Also photographed was the funeral procession through Kirkby Stephen and the communal grave in the cemetery there.

Across the County Border

Servants of the Railway

AT GARSDALE, No 13 Railway Cottages was also a Temperance Hotel, kept by Mr and Mrs Reuben Alton, who accomodated rail-users, mostly commercial travellers. In this row, as recently as 1945, water needed for household use was collected from a pump or even the local gill. Not until the early 1950s were the residents at Garsdale provided with a piped water supply.

The Tank House became a focal-point of social life over a wide area! It was an unglamorous structure, just an iron tank holding 80,000 gallons of water, supported on lofty walls made of dressed stone. (The Tank House was demolished in 1971).

From just after the first world war until the coming of television caused interest in rural events to dwindle, the folk of Garsdale Head used the Tank House as a centre for domino and whist drives, potato pie suppers and concerts. Cheerful volunteers converted the single-room building in 1918, "a tin roof" being fitted within for comfort and warmth. The cost of materials was met by the £25 raised at a dance held in the school. By visiting sales, it was possible to purchase cheaply some planks for the floor and for making seats; a gramophone, a piano and lamps. The place was brightly decorated.

Music for dancing was usually provided by a pianist and accordionist. Then a small band, two accordions and drums, was formed.

Mrs Curtis, a teacher at Lunds, was one of the regular visiting musicians, but anyone who could play a musical instrument was welcome to play. A former stationmaster with musical ability would have liked to expand the scope of the music, complaining that most of the farmers and their wives would consider only olde-tyme" dances. "They won't look at the samba and modern stuff, perhaps because we haven't enough young people to set an example."

Platelayers clear snow from the points, Aisgill, 1947.

At the Tank House, the "wallflowers" sat on red-upholstered seats that had been taken from a scrapped railway carriage. The buffet was a wheelless railway carriage of Midland ancestry. Some of the events held in the Tank House raised up to £40 for the Bradford Royal Infirmary.

A former signalman told me: "When we came to Garsdale in 1934, the Tank House dances were attended by farm folk and railway folk. There was little else to do at Garsdale at the time. They were good dances. Sixpenny hops, they called them. The pianist for some of the 'hops' was Alice Scarr, of the *Moorcock.* At other dances, the pianist would be Isobel Gamsby, from Grizedale Crossing. Everybody joined in.

The dance floor was improved when some of the men bought a heap of railway sleepers, using them to cover the old floor. Over the sleepers they fitted tongued and grooved boards. "It was just like a skating rink at times!"

The buffet carriage was set endways on to the building; inside this carriage there was just a couple of long tables and some chairs, with "a bit of a kitchen" at one end. Water was heated on a coke stove. It is easy to scoff at the facilities, but this building had originally been a draughty room with stone floor, used mainly for tools.

People cannot live by dancing alone. In 1938, there was one small shop near the station so the LMS granted a free pass each week to a railwayman's wife so that she might visit the market at Hawes or at Settle, 20 miles away.

Garsdalians with a fancy for reading—and rail passengers with a long wait at the station in prospect—might borrow a book from the library. A journalist wrote: "If it is in the daytime—and if you have an honest face—you can go into the waiting room and perhaps the Stationmaster will lend you a book from the unique library there."

At the turn of the century, about 150 books, mainly of the Victorian "improving" kind, were presented to the station by two elderly ladies from Wensleydale who often travelled through Garsdale—or Hawes Junction as it then was—and felt sorry for the railwaymen who lived miles from anywhere.

The books were handed into the charge of the Stationmaster; he became the chief librarian. They were to be lent out free to the staff. In 1938, when Stationmaster at Garsdale was J.F. Ferguson, some modern fiction was added to the original stock of books. The library was still reported as being "spick and span" in 1945. Now the books were being kept in the ladies waiting room. The waiting room on the "down" platform, having been a chapel, still contained the organ and "a few moth-eaten hymn books."

A sad sight as the interior of the water tower at Garsdale is demolished. It was in this relatively confined space that railwaymen and dalesfolk managed to find room to dance.

Summertime at Garsdale was for gardening, either growing vegetables to eke out the family income by producing cheap food or tending flowers, as did Douglas Cobb, the stationmaster I met on a visit in 1953. He had started a platform garden, importing the soil. He grew flowers on windswept platforms over 1,000 feet above sea level.

The Bleak Midwinter

GARSDALE is exposed to all the winds that blow—winds that may reach a velocity of 100 miles an hour. At such times— so I was once assured—the signalman in the Garsdale box might feel his chair moving beneath him.

In the early part of 1947, when the Settle-Carlisle was blocked for about six weeks, the branch was kept open and along the rails came rations for the people of Garsdale, who would otherwise have gone hungry.

The Garsdale water troughs, just to the north of Rise Hill, had to be tended round the clock when there was a keen frost. The troughs were fed by water from a 43,000 gallon storage tank which received a supply by pipe from a reservoir on the hillside above. Harry Cox, who worked on the installation of the troughs in 1907—they cost £4,396—told me that when the hillside reservoir was made, a stream was diverted and a gang of between 50 and 60 men set about making a concrete dam, conveying materials across the fell on a light railway.

"George Fawcett was the man in charge, with Bill Smith as the ganger. It took nearly 12 months to construct the dam, during which time water was diverted over the top along a chute. When the day came to use the dam, some 'top brass' turned up. The water was allowed back into its old course, and the dam leaked like a sieve because the cement had not set properly.

In fact, not enough cement was used. Someone had been trying to save the Midland Company a little money. The work had to be done again."

Aisgill: the great snow of 1947

(photographs from local albums)

Harry continued: "To instal the troughs, rails were removed and the top soil dug out. Then slag from a steel works was put in the trenches; the slag was full of holes, like a sponge. We dug down for two or three feet. . . When the first locomotives used the troughs, folks gathered to watch 'em, as folks will. But the scoops were not working properly; they simply pushed the water out, and sightseers were soaked to the skin. A device was added to the scoops so that it would 'cut' into the water."

A Carlisle driver observed: "You hadn't to put the scoop in too far, and you had to get it out as quickly as you could, or it flooded over. It came up through the gauge in the cab and soaked the crew."

Big Bass was driving with a plough one day when the troughs were frozen solid, and the snow had become packed on top of the ice. "Off he set, but instead of hitting and going into the snow, the plough rode up, the engines following. They ended up crossways, blocking both main lines and about four feet from going down the bank into the Dent Valley."

Steam-heating was introduced at the lineside to ensure a flow of water to the troughs. Dick Fawcett recalled that, in cold snaps, "steam—raisers" came from the Hellifield Shed. The troughs needed attention when any spilled water immediately froze hard. Ice, which also covered the track and sleepers, had to be broken up and removed by men using picks and shovels. "We all wore clogs in those days. I could never really walk properly in these, let alone stand and work on the side of a sloping ice-field."

Railwaymen maintained that the troughs were unreliable, freezing over in winter, drying up in summer and being blocked by fallen leaves in autumn. They were only available for use in spring! In the 1950s, it was decided to remove the troughs for maintenance, after which they would be re-fixed.

At that time they were made of steel, in lengths, bolted together, with perhaps 24 bolts in a joint. Dick remembered that some rubber had been inserted in the joints. "It was early autumn when we set to work on the troughs. We had a big gang, with men recruited from Carlisle to Skipton. Most of them were lodging in houses round about. . . The troughs were heavy; it was as much as we could do to get them to the side of the line for maintenance. We did some work on the dam on the hillside, though we should have done more."

Garsdale water troughs as seen from the footplate (looking back!) of a BR standard Class 4 locomotive. Of particular note is the Midland Railway distant signal, which fortunately is still in use.

AISGILL
SUMMIT
1,169 FEET

Main photograph: Class 5 No. 44932 coas down from Aisgill summit, June, 1991. *Top, le* Aisgill box, now at Butterley, Derbyshire. Middl A Midland 4-4-0 passes the site of the Aisg crash in 1913. *Bottom, left:* ''Evening Sta makes a spirited attack on Aisgill summit. *Rigl* A Class 4 takes a breather at the Aisgill box whi hauling a local ''trip'' working.

BRITISH RAILWAYS

Garsdale Today

THE JUNCTION ceased to exist in 1959 with the closing of the Wensleydale line; the stopping service for passenger trains on the Settle-Carlisle ended at Garsdale in May, 1970, leaving *Dalesrail* to sustain a service of sorts. The platforms have been stripped of much of their interest, such as two drinking fountains, one dated 1873 and the other 1880.

In the report entitled *Interpreting the Heritage of the Settle-Carlisle railway line,* prepared for the Countryside Commission by the Centre of Enviromental Interpretation, Manchester Polytechnic (1985), prominence is given to a suggestion that a visitor centre should be established at Garsdale station.

"There is the need for a focal point for activity and interpretation at a station along the line which can be reached in an hour or so from Carlisle and Settle, at which both special and regular trains stop and which can be reached by car. Garsdale is by far the most popular station for *Dales Rail* users and is near the junction of the A684 and B6259."

With its splendid setting, and its ability to water thirsty "steamers", Garsdale still attracts the crowds.

Glory of Steam: Past and Present

Opposite page: A newcomer to the Settle-Carlisle—No. 46203, "Princess Margaret Rose"— waits on a June day in 1991 for the moment to depart from Garsdale to Carlisle with "The Midlander". *This page:* Artist's impression of a Jubilee, No. 5660 "Rooke", climbing Aisgill in October, 1937, on a record run, which justified the modification of the original design to suit the expresses of the day. The Jubilee's performance in 1937, when its relatively small size is taken into account, gives it a special place in the annals of British steam.

The Train Now Departing . . .

No. 46203, "Princess Margaret Rose", heads for Dandry Mire Viaduct on its way to Carlisle with 11 coaches full of excited travellers.